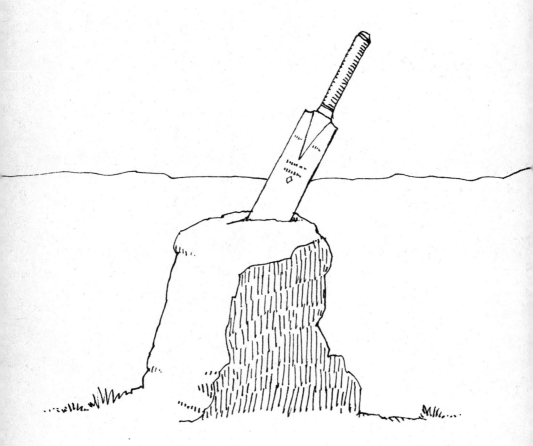

SIMON BOND

Stroked Through the Covers

A Methuen Paperback

A METHUEN PAPERBACK

First published in Great Britain in 1987
by Methuen London Ltd
11 New Fetter Lane, London EC4P 4EE
Copyright © Polycarp Ltd 1987
Made and printed in Great Britain

British Library Cataloguing in Publication Data

Bond, Simon
   Stroked through the covers.
   1. English wit and humor, Pictorial
   I. Title
   741.5′942   NC1479

   ISBN 0-413-14170-5
       0-413-16910-3 (Hardback)

For anyone who has ever dropped a catch.

~AND ON THE SEVENTH DAY GOD INVENTED CRICKET~

THE FIRST BOUNCER

THE FULL DRESS UNIFORM OF A CRICKET SUPPORTER

ENGLISH

AUSTRALIAN

SYLVESTER STALLONE IN THE CRICKET MATCH

HE BOWLED.. AND HE BOWLED TO KILL!

'Let's try a leg-break against the right tower first, shall we?'

FOR GODS SAKE—TRY DIBLEY FROM THE PAVILION END

CHARACTERS OF THE GAME

FitzGibbon 'Nodder' MacLaren
ENGLAND, DORSET AND ST. BARTS HOSPITAL

Famous throughout the County game between the Wars for heading short pitched balls to third man

His best innings was 138 n.o. with 102 coming off his head.

He also scored 36 in his second innings, but could not remember a thing till the following March.

On his death he donated his body to science. And when last sighted his forehead was being used as a door stop at the Rumba Rumba Club, Soho.

Terrence 'Lightning' Topley

CHARTERHOUSE, SURREY AND BRITISH RAIL

The slowest left arm spin bowler ever in English cricket. Even Jessop once hitting him at full power, just managed to get the ball to the covers.

Most of Topley's wickets came from batsmen's frustration or dislocated shoulders.

He was never seen to run on or off the cricket field. And once in a fit of pique stamped his foot. Which was so out of character that it was reported in The Times. He played well into his sixties and reputedly bowled faster then than in his twenties.

He chewed all his food 24 times before swallowing. He never drank and was acknowledged to be the most boring man in S.London.

Sir Dudley Emerson-Evans

HARROW, DEVONSHIRE AND THE RITZ RESTAURANT

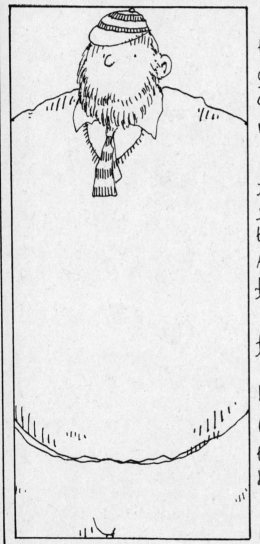

Considered the fattest man to play first-class cricket. Only given out L.B.W. 4 times in his career, mostly because no one knew where the wicket was.

Only 8% of his runs came from non-boundary strokes. In his youth, Emerson-Evans once tried to run a 3 to deep extra cover. Afterwards he needed to lie down for 2 days to recover.

He always referred to his good friend W.G. Grace as 'Titch'.

He usually fielded directly behind the bowler on the boundary. Mostly to save running, but also to give the batsman a good background to see the ball.

He retired in 1880 and later became a local landmark.

Evelyn Sacheverell de Grymmes

KILLARNEY ACADEMY, SANDHURST & H.M. PRISON DURHAM

Acknowledged as the nastiest person to ever play club cricket.

He was asked to leave more clubs than any other single person.

Mostly, for his appalling behaviour and vicious reaction towards umpires.

His average for assaults was even higher than that for runs. And only slightly lower than that for bowling. The number of batsmen injured by his bowling was so high, that the whole of the British medical profession begged for his banning.

His only friend seems to have been Archduke Franz Ferdinand of Austria. And it is considered by some that the ~~assassination~~ of the Archduke was actually meant for de Grymmes, who ducked at the right time, just avoiding the M.C.C.'s hitman's bullet.

(In later years de Grymmes went mad and became a newspaper proprietor).

NEW UMPIRING SIGNALS

SUPPORTERS ADVANCING — PLEASE HELP

THERE'S A PLAYER DRUNK ON THE FIELD

THE COMMENTATORS ARE TALKING TWADDLE

'I AM IN PHYSICAL DISCOMFORT.'

HAROLD
LARWOOD

NOTTS
&
ENGLAND

EVOLUTION OF THE CRICKET BALL

S. ENGLAND	YORK	KENT	KENT & SUSSEX
495 B.C.	1200 A.D.	1400 A.D.	1570 A.D.
ROCK	WOOD	LEATHER AROUND SAND	LEATHER & WOOD
LONDON	NOTTS.	LONDON	MELBOURNE
1600 A.D.	1750 A.D.	1840 A.D.	1986 A.D.
TWINE AROUND BONE	LEATHER AROUND COAL	LEATHER & COMPOSITE	ROCK

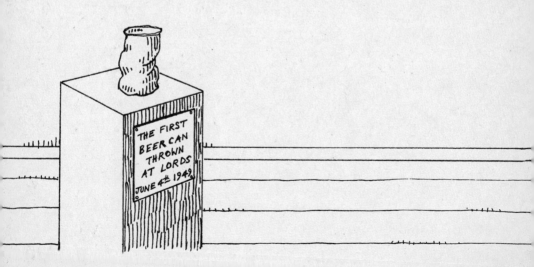

THE FIRST
BEER CAN
THROWN
AT LORDS
JUNE 4th 1949

DIFFERENT DELIVERIES

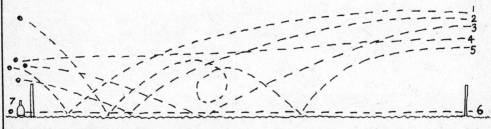

1. THE OVER PITCHED DELIVERY
2. THE PERFECT DELIVERY
3. THE SHORT DELIVERY
4. THE NASTY DELIVERY
5. THE ODD DELIVERY
6. THE CHAPPELL DELIVERY
7. THE MILK DELIVERY

How to handle spin............P.T.O.

THE JOEL GARNER GUEST XI TAKE TO THE FIELD

'Isn't there something about this in the Geneva Convention?'

THE M.C.C. TOURING SIDE
SICILY 1949

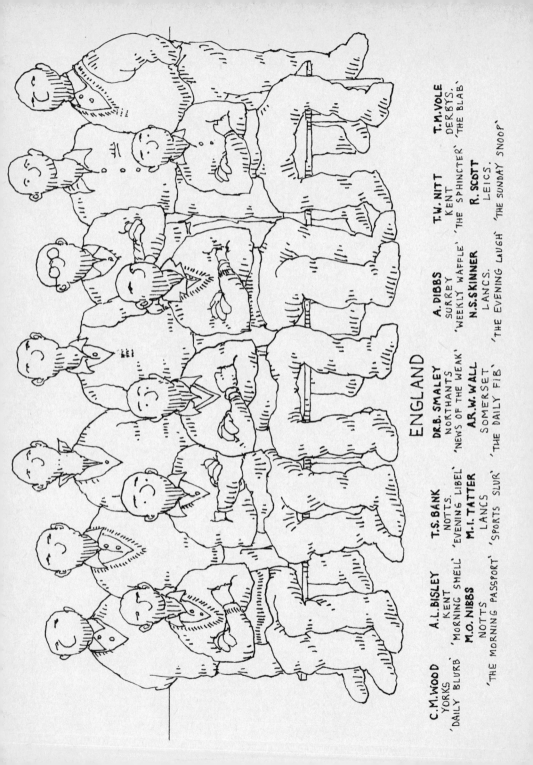

ENGLAND

C.M.WOOD
YORKS
'DAILY BLURB'

A.L.BISLEY
KENT
'MORNING SMELL'

M.O.NIBBS
NOTTS
'THE MORNING PASSPORT'

T.S.BANK
NOTTS.
'EVENING LIBEL'

M.I.TATTER
LANCS
'SPORTS SLUR'

DR.B.SMALEY
NORTHANTS
'NEWS OF THE WEAK'

A.R.W.WALL
SOMERSET
'THE DAILY FIB'

A.DIBBS
SURREY
'WEEKLY WAFFLE'

N.S.SKINNER
LANCS.
'THE EVENING LAUGH'

T.W.NITT
KENT
'THE SPHINCTER'

R.SCOTT
LEICS.
'THE SUNDAY SNOOP'

T.M.VOLE
DERBYS.
'THE BLAB'

'I don't mind bowling a little later, Skip . . . say about June.'

'Oh, my God . . . Hammond's out!'

'And Dibley drives past mid-off for two . . .
he's timing his front foot shots well today isn't he, Brian?'

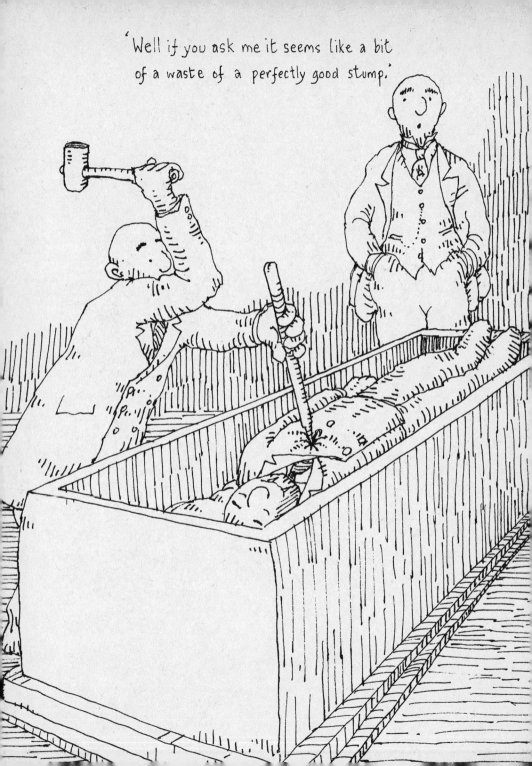

'So the score before lunch is Australia 183 for 4 . . .
and Lionel is 6 not out.'

THE 'TWICE TWIRL SURPRISE' SEAMER..... FIRST USED BY HUGO HOADLEY-WEST 1922

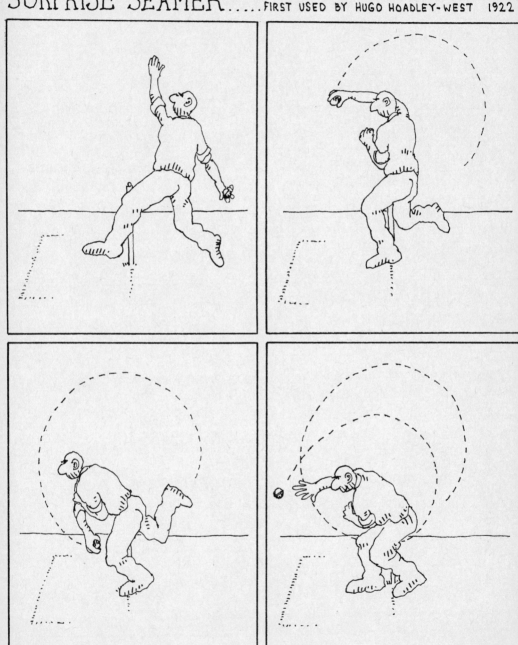

The Short Pitched Ball — and how to handle it.

THE MARCH OF TIME

'Have you noticed how all the umpires seem to be getting younger?'

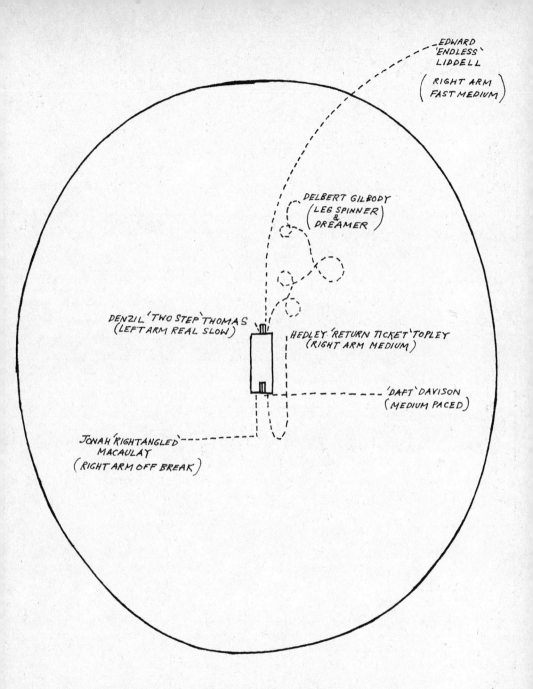

EDWARD
'ENDLESS'
LIDDELL

(RIGHT ARM
FAST MEDIUM)

DELBERT GILBODY
(LEG SPINNER)
&
(DREAMER)

DENZIL 'TWO STEP' THOMAS
(LEFT ARM REAL SLOW)

HEDLEY 'RETURN TICKET' TOPLEY
(RIGHT ARM MEDIUM)

'DAFT' DAVISON
(MEDIUM PACED)

JONAH 'RIGHTANGLED'
MACAULAY
(RIGHT ARM OFF BREAK)

REMARKABLE RUN-UPS
1890 - 1940

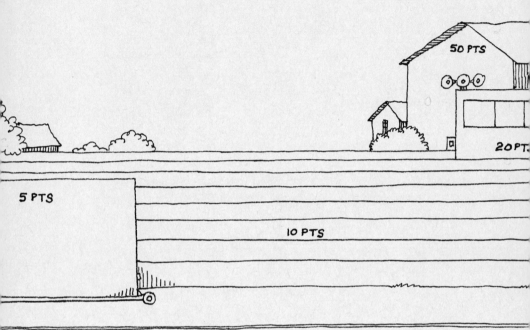

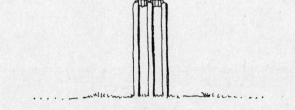

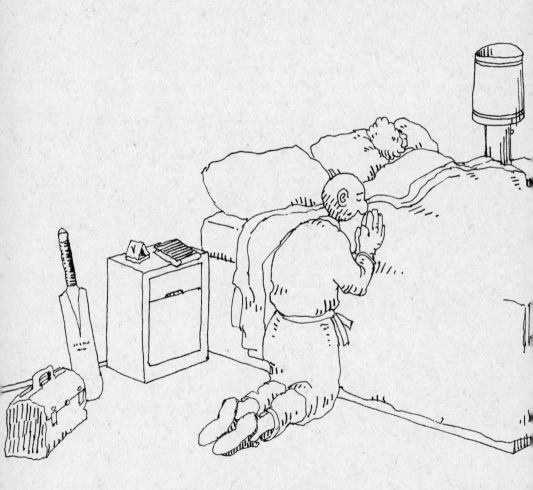

'. . . and please, please, please,
no short risers on middle and leg.'

'I see Botham's batting again.'

BAD NEWS FROM THE WEST INDIES

'And finally, gentlemen,
Miss Silverman with the lunch-time scores.'

'. . . and finally, Middlesex are 120 for 3 . . .'

'Miss Lemon, I'm your boss,
this is my company and you're out, OK!'

AN EXCITING DAY AT TUNBRIDGE WELLS

BIZARRE SCORE CARDS No. 9

JUNE 24th 1948

NIPLEY COOMBE v BROADMOOR ROVERS XI

J.R. DIMBLE	BOWLED SIMMONS	14
P.R. O'CONNOR	LBW BOWLED RODGERS	3
S. ALSOP	HIT WICKET	1
W.R. NITT	HIT WICKET	11
J.H.P. LITLY-NOBBS	HIT BOWLER	4
S.P. FLYNN	HIT UMPIRE	8
D.F. METCALF	HIT SELF	6
M.I. METCALF	HIT W'KEEPER & SLIPS	11
J. CRUMP	HIT SCOREBOARD	2
M.T. LOWLY-LUMMLEY	HIT PAVILION AND GENTS TOILET	3
I. TODDY	HIT OTHER BATSMAN AND THEN A STRAY DOG	0
P. O'ROURKE	NOT OUT (BUT SLIGHTLY HURT)	2
EXTRAS	0	TOTAL 55

'. . . *and they found his box forty yards behind second slip.*'

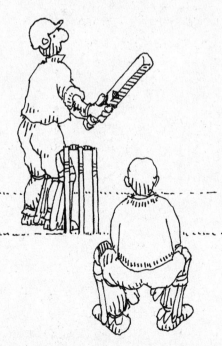

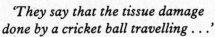

*'They say that the tissue damage
done by a cricket ball travelling . . .'*

'...so he got his century all right ...
but they never found the ball ...'

*'. . . so he went for the return catch . . .
and it took three weeks for the blood stains to disappear.'*

'Of course he held the catch,
but he never played the piano again.'

'Mind you, I once saw Randall catch one like that
one-handed whilst signing an autograph . . .'

'By the way, I've got the negatives
of you and the Chairman's wife in a safe place.'

 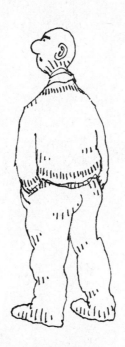

*'So finally the MCC phoned me
and told me I'd been right all along.'*

'Take it easy, Fenway, there's still two Tests left!'

'. . . and what about the LBW decision on August 19th 1973 . . .?'

AUBREY ST. JOHN
LASCELLES
1863~1940

THE INVENTOR
OF THE
CRICKET BOX

'Fast for a spinner, isn't he?'

ALTERNATIVE FIELDING POSITIONS

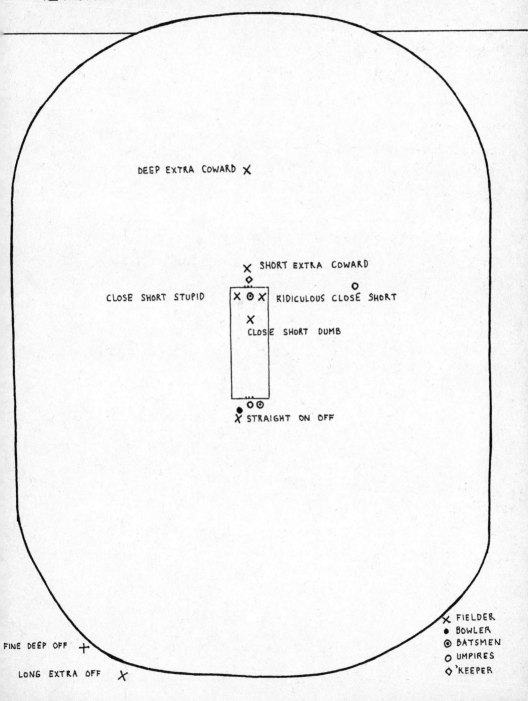

THE BATSMAN'S DAY-DREAM
Second day of this majestic innings...runs in all areas and at a cracking pace... the W. Indies quicks have been hammered...a truly great spectacle... an historic innings.. and a privilege to be here...

THE BOWLER'S DAY-DREAM

..and once more the long, lean muscled body of Edwards walks back menacingly...again Australia in terrible trouble.. ...18 for 6 ...again almost unplayable...and even better than in the first innings....

THE HIGHEST SCORE
EVER RECORDED

26,492 for 0

Mr. Trevor Wimbledon Worthing, SUSSEX

Was scored by a Mr Trevor Wimbledon of Worthing, Sussex in 1966 in his back garden off the bowling of his four-year-old son Gary. The five day match was called a draw when Gary (2 not out) retired hurt from a short ball which ricocheted off a garden spade and removed Gary from the crease. And also from the garden.

The following year Trevor Wimbledon scored 19,112 also against his son (now five).

In 1979 the now fully grown Gary murdered his father with the self same spade. And against the non-existent bowling of his now dead father scored 83,722 n.o. in a period of 3 weeks before imprisonment.

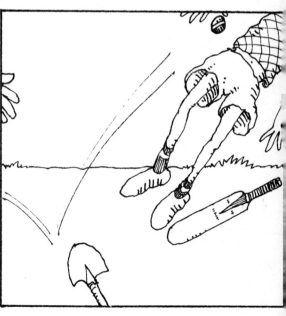

THE HIGHEST SCORE
EVER RECORDED
(FIRST CLASS MATCHES)

The Nawab of Nimani

The Nawab of Nimani's XI in 1928 in a match against the Nawab of Nimani's Household XI scored 2741 for 0 in a 3 day Inter-Zone match.

The match was abandoned after 298 L.B.W., 108 caught, 74 run out and 8 hit wicket appeals were turned down by the umpires (the Nawab of Nimani and the Nawab of Nimani).

Of the 2741 runs scored, 1840 were scored by the Nawab of Nimani himself.

During the following years all the games between the two above teams ended in similar circumstances. Fortunately, the Nawab lost interest in cricket and turned his attention to basketball. And not suprisingly, in 1934 the Nawab of Nimani's 'A' team beat the Nawab of Nimani's 'B' team by the still record score of 482 points against 14 points.

Luckily, he died before he discovered football.

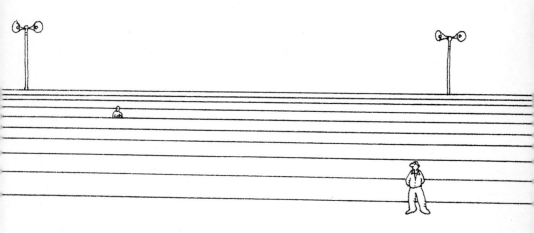

'Will the gentleman wearing the hat
please stop crunching his crisps.'

PLAYERS TO AVOID

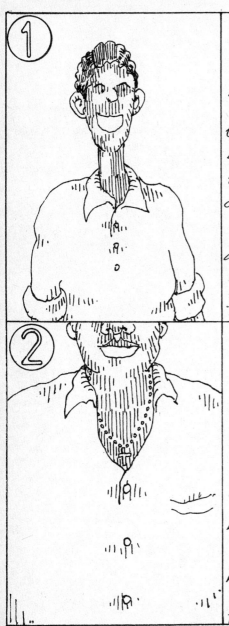

①

Any slightly built and charming Indian batsmen who seem very young, slim and frail.

Who always seem to have scored their first first-class hundred against Indian Railways when they were twelve. And their first double century in the next innings.

Beware of their endless concentration and languid shots. And also beware of their brothers and brothers-in-law. Second cousins, nephews, aunts...

②

Any large, fast and untutored bowlers whom people in Barbados call a bit 'quick'. And who tell you that their heroes are always other famous 'quickies'. Who have a deep-rooted desire to play in England and especially against them.

They usually have very English names and like to bat a bit, too.

Always, extremely pleasant off the field. However, once on....

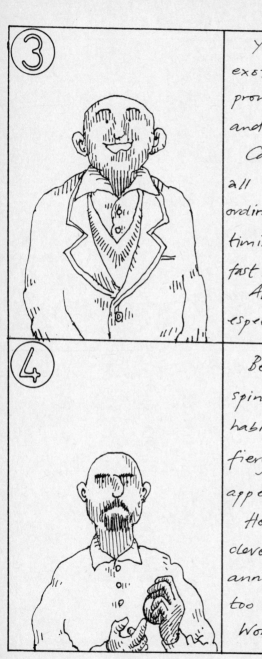

3

Young Sri Lankan batsmen with exotic and difficult names to pronounce, Who enjoy batting and want to prove themselves.

Can be any shape, except they all look like teenagers and rather ordinary. However, seem to have superb timing and quite enjoy facing the fast bowlers, 'as the ball goes farther'.

Always ready to enjoy themselves, especially at a bowler's expense.

4

Be very wary of small, oddly named spin bowlers with very idiocyncratic habits and delivery. Quite often fiery tempered and ebullient appealers. Especially in Urdu.

However, they are cunning and clever. And do have a rather annoying habit of scoring runs too when needed.

Wonderful to watch. Awful to play.

⑤

Raw-boned and strong lads from the Outback. Who used to practice bowling at one stump back at home. Hour after hour after hour.

Not normally controlled bowlers, but love to push it through rather fast. And don't mind putting in a few short ones. Just for fun.

They also enjoy a bit of a whack. And quite often whack it quite well, dammit.

⑥

Any bloody Kiwi who comes from a family of sportsmen. Especially if they persist in telling you how they hunger for the quiet life. And later quieten everyone, amidst the 'crash of ash' and the fall of egos.

Who also constantly tell you how much they enjoy playing in England. Especially early on in the day, when the ball moves a bit. And so do we — mostly back to the pavilion and a crossword.

THE M.C.C. CELEBRATE A
FAMOUS VICTORY

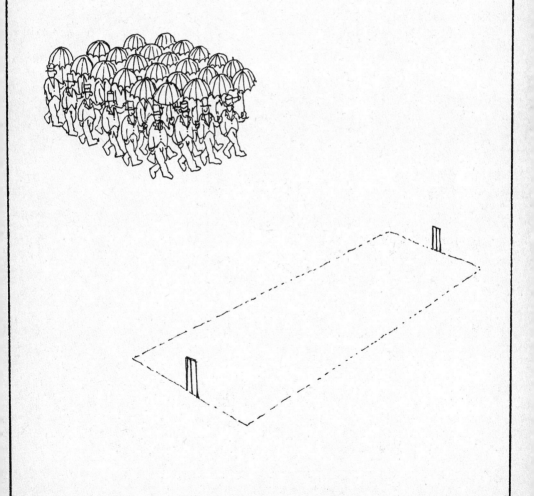

ENGLAND v WEST INDIES

(every little bit helps)

CATCHING THEM YOUNG

'. . . seven maidens, four wickets for sixty . . .'

Recommended Reading~

SEX AND THE SWING BOWLER
DEMPSEY GONADS

COMMUNISM AND THE COVER DRIVE
Senator Kelvin O'Connor (N.S.W.)

FIRED UP FOR THE ASHES
BERNARD BLANDLY
LOTS OF PHOTOGRAPHS NOT MANY WORDS

TEAM SPIRIT
Geoffrey Boycott

WISDEN
BOOK OF ENDLESS TABLES AND TINY PRINTING
EDITED BY NORMAN BORING

STRAIGHT BAT TO HELL
Rev. Arthur Wurtley Hargreaves
Cricket and the Anti-Christ

CRICKET ETIQUETTE
DENNIS LILLEE

THE ART OF UNDERARM BOWLING
GREG & TREVOR CHAPPELL

'Oh, damn . . . well, I suppose that means no play after tea.'

A WIDE WIDE

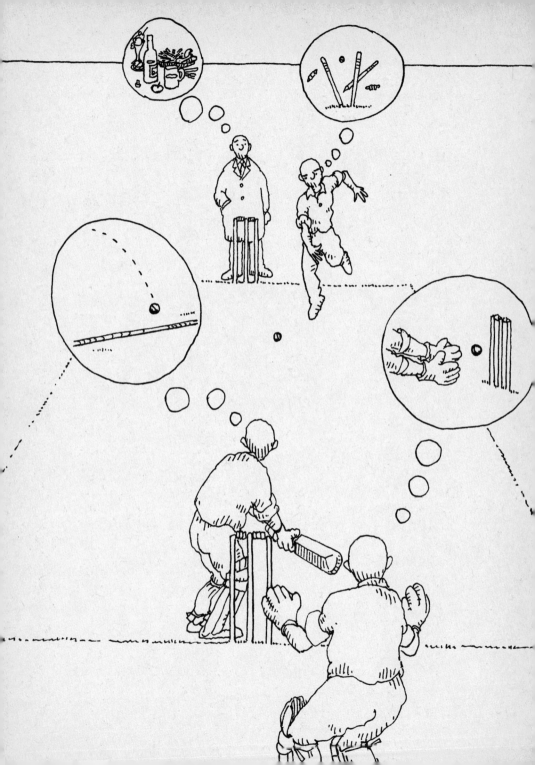

HOW TO HANDLE A FAST BOWLER

TAKING GUARD

THE PESSIMIST

'Somewhere about three feet outside leg stump if you please, umpire.'

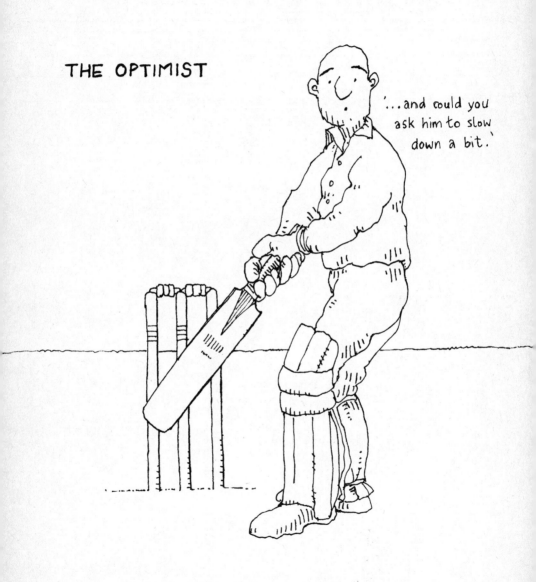

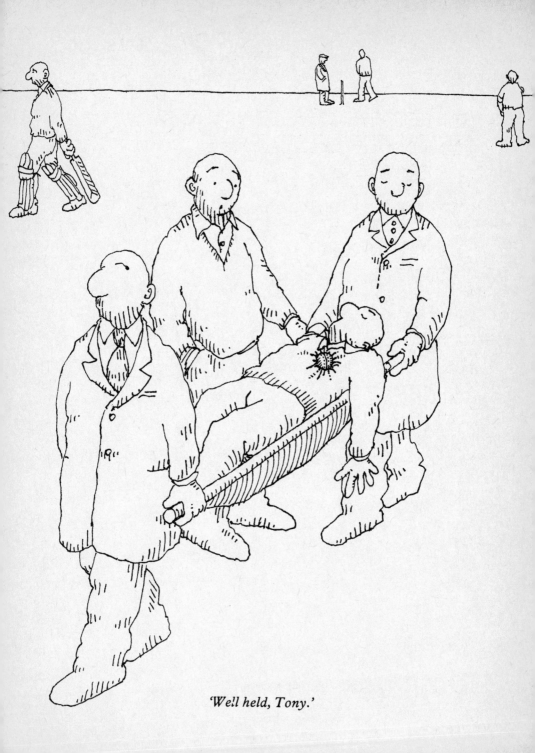

'Well held, Tony.'

'And with this one I scored 138 not out . . .
every one off the edge.'

THE M.C.C. PICKS THE TEAM FOR AUSTRALIA

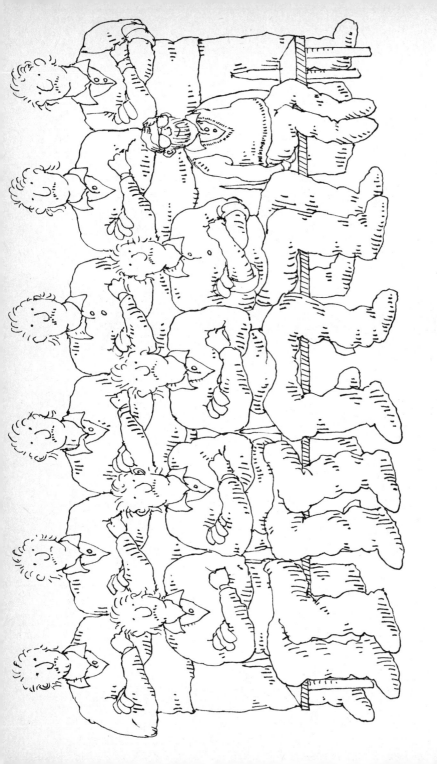

THE PERFECT ENGLAND XI

I.T.BOTHAM I.T.BOTHAM I.T.BOTHAM I.T.BOTHAM I.T.BOTHAM

I.T.BOTHAM I.T.BOTHAM I.T.BOTHAM I.T.BOTHAM ME

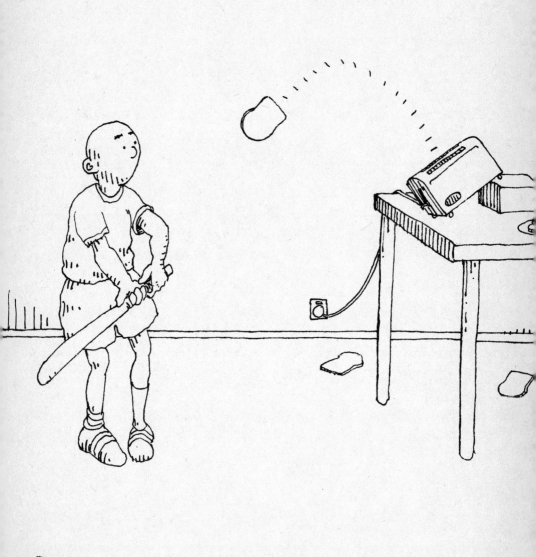

THE FINAL OUT

THE END

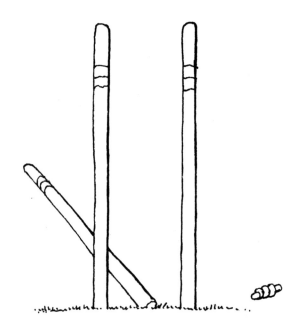